Growing Up with Granny

Lora Goff

11-4-21
To Westfield friends
Hope all enjoy
the stories—
Lora Goff

Published by Pen It! Publications, LLC
812-371-4128 www.penitpublications.com

ISBN: 978-1-951263-58-4

Edited by Wanda Williams
Cover by Donna Cook

Dedication

This book is dedicated to my late husband, Rollie. He was my constant support, always listening to my writings and encouraging me to keep going.

To our four children: Myrna Molter, Gary Goff, Maria Ging, and Melanie Hoff, who are my forever loved ones and my constant joy.

And to my grandchildren: Heather Garrett, Alayna Ging, Trey Hoff, Tori Hoff, Jacob Molter, and Noah Molter who show their love for me in so many ways. I can't forget my two great grandchildren: Isaiah Garrett and Felicity Garrett who have listened to many of Granny's stories offering their thoughts.

And to my former elementary students who continue to share with me as they have grown and gone on with their lives.

Last, but certainly not least, to the Discipleship Class of the Sheridan Six Points Wesleyan Church, as we studied the Word of God.

Acknowledgments

This book could never have reached publication without the help of others. There are those I consider my tech gurus: Ron Stone, Maria Ging, Cheri Hume, Janet Bragg, and Scott Garrett. Thank you for your many hours.

Special mention to author, Kristen Lehr, who also helped me learn to navigate the technology involved. Having taught computer at first grade level, I found myself woefully lacking in the fast-paced technology of today's world.

A special thanks to Kirk Green who encouraged me to start blogging my writings. And a very grateful thanks to all who inspired me along the way as I continued to write.

And above all, praise and glory to my God who has showered me with so many blessings!

Contents

Introduction

Granny grew up in a different time.

A time when people pumped water from the well outside to bathe and drink.

A time when families made homemade ice cream on hot, summer nights.

A time when children played Hide and Seek and Kick the Can in the dark.

A time when there were no cell phones, no computers, no video games, no

IPads, and very few TVs.

A time when winter snows meant sledding on the hill and ice skating.

A time when the summer sun beckoned us to the woods to play along the creek.

A time when we rode our bike, climbed trees, and swam in the horse tank.

A time when everyone had chores to do and yet always had time for fun.

Sounds like a long time ago, doesn't it? In this book, you will see that many of the things Granny did are much like what you do. She shares what it was like growing up on a farm long ago. Granny shares the lessons she learned, making her the kind of person

God wanted her to be. Granny hopes that as you listen to, or read the stories, you will get to know about God who loves you very much. And how He is always teaching you lessons in life so that you will be the kind of person God wants you to be.

Love,
Granny

One Scary Night

Psalm 56:3
"Whenever I am afraid, I will trust in You."

It had been a good day, but it would soon be over. The evening shadows were falling quickly around the big, three story brick house we had recently moved into. I was eight years old and I felt fear in my heart. I knew my two sisters and I would soon have to go to bed in this strange and scary house that had no electricity.

When the call for "Bedtime" finally came, we followed Mom up the long, dark, and winding staircase. She carried a kerosene lamp (that was our light) so we could make our way safely. We crept up slowly watching the dark shadows dancing on the wall and following us up the stairway.

Mom tucked us in bed and told us a short story and then had to leave and take care of our little brother and sister. She took the light with her when she told us goodnight. Terror is the only word to describe our feelings. All we could think of were the shadows that followed us and where were they now? We dove under the covers and began to sing quietly

"Jesus loves me, this I know..." Surely, He would protect us. We finally dropped off to sleep.

Since I have grown up, and learned about shadows, I have also learned how God watches over me. So, when I'm afraid, I just trust Him to keep me safe.

1. Have you ever been afraid?

2. What were the shadows on the wall?

3. Did you know you can pray and ask God to keep you and your family safe?

Good and Bad Fruit

Matthew 7:17
   "...Every good tree bears good fruit, but a bad tree bears bad fruit."

Strawberries ripened first in the summer. I loved strawberries. When picking, we had to be careful not to step on the leaves. It seemed like those bright red strawberries always hid under the leaves. Of course, I had to eat a few as I picked. They were so warm, ripe, and tasty. But after picking and eating those yummy berries for a few days, I woke up to a rash of hives all over my body. My legs would itch, my arms would itch, my nose would itch. I couldn't scratch fast enough. I learned that year not to overeat something just because it tasted good.

   God compares us to a tree that bears good fruit. He wants us to share his love, joy, peace, and caring with others. These are some of God's good fruits.

1. Did you share the fruit of love today?

2. Can a smile be good fruit?

3. Can you name what might be a bad fruit?

Planting the Garden

Philippians 4:19
 "And my God shall supply all your need according to His riches in glory by Christ Jesus."

The spring rains had passed and the ground in the garden was ready for Dad to plow. Farmers call it tilling the soil. I loved the smell of the dirt as the plow turned it over and over. Mom had bought many vegetable seeds and onion sets. There were radishes, carrots, peas, cauliflower, cucumbers, corn, beets, tomatoes, and green beans. It always surprised me how those little seeds grew into enough food to feed our big family.

Once the seeds were planted in the ground, there was much more work to be done. We had to hoe the dirt around the plants. That gave them air and helped them grow faster and bigger. We had to be careful not to hurt the plant. Then we had to watch for weeds and pull them. And at last the day came when we began to harvest our garden. Some of the vegetables were ready to pick before others. We helped Mom pick beans and snap them into small pieces. She would can them in jars for our winter meals. They tasted so good we forgot about how hard we worked.

1.   Why did Dad have to plow up the dirt in the garden?

2.   What makes the seeds grow?

3.   Do you have a favorite vegetable you like to eat?

Think Before You Act

Ephesians 4:32
    "And be kind to one another, tenderhearted, forgiving one another, even as God in Christ forgave you."

The day was finally here. Our cousins were coming to play. What fun we would have playing house in our corncrib playhouse. But something went wrong. The old devil came along and brought jealousy and selfishness with him. That's the way he does. He sneaks around and messes up the plans we have for a good time.

My cousin Jackie and I were the oldest in our two families. We began to argue over who was going to be boss. *She was so bossy,* I thought. When we went outside, I picked a handful of cockle burrs, (those are very sticky little plants) and plopped them right smack dab on top of her head. She had really curly hair and those cockle burrs stuck tight. Oh, was I ever in trouble!

Jackie and I laugh about this now that we are older, but we weren't being very kind to each other at the time. We should have remembered that God wanted both of us to be kind and loving. Granny certainly didn't think before she acted. I hope you will remember this special verse when you start to say something unkind or do something that might hurt another person.

1.   Name 5 things you can do to show kindness.

2.   When you and your friend or cousin start to argue, what should you do?

3.   How do you feel when you have acted selfish or jealous?

Free to Speak

Acts 4:20
"For we cannot but speak the things which we have seen and heard."

Anna was telling her friends about her Dad. He was a fireman. He went into burning buildings and saved lives and tried to keep people's homes from burning. The older boy next door came over and heard her talking about her Dad. He got very angry and told Anna he didn't want to hear any more stories about her Dad. He was a little jealous, because his Dad was never home.

In the Bible, the High Priest and the other rulers told Jesus' disciples not to be talking about Jesus and all the wonderful miracles He had performed. The rulers commanded them, saying, "Do not speak at all or teach in the Name of Jesus." These men were like Anna's neighbor. They didn't want to hear it. I think they were jealous too. We do not have to let others tell us we can't talk about the good things our Dad and Mom do. And we shouldn't let anyone tell us not to praise God for all the things

He does for us. He is a good God and He loves us with an everlasting love.

1. Do you think Anna's neighbor thought she was bragging?

2. Is it okay to share with others what your parents do to help you and to help others?

3. Do you feel jealous sometimes? How can you overcome being jealous?

The Night Jesus Was Born

Luke 2:11

"For there is born to you this day in the city of David a Savior, who is Christ the Lord."

We will soon be celebrating Jesus' birth. I wonder what it was like a long, long time ago in that little town of Bethlehem. The Bible tells us many people had come from far away to pay their taxes. Everyone was hot and tired and looking for a place to stay. Joseph and Mary, Jesus' parents, were also looking for a place to rest and sleep.

There were no hospitals like we have today. They wanted to find a good place for Jesus to be born. When they could find no room, the innkeeper told them to go to his stable just outside of town.

On that night long ago, there were shepherds out in the fields watching over their sheep. The Angel of the Lord came to them and told them something wonderful had happened. "To you is born this day in the city of David, a Savior, which is Christ the Lord." The Angel even told them they would find the baby wrapped in swaddling clothes lying in a manger. And

23

then, thousands of angels came and began to sing and praise God.

God sent His very own Son into the world as a little baby boy. A very special Gift. And He did it just for you and for me. And for all other boys and girls. For moms and dads, and grannies and grandpas. That's why we celebrate Christmas.

1. What does Christmas mean to you?

2. Why do you think the angels began to sing and praise God?

3. Have you accepted Jesus into your heart?

Riding the Bus

Psalm 36:7

"How precious is Your lovingkindness, O God!"

School bells are ringing. How excited you must be. Will you be riding a bus to school? If you do, I hope you and your friends enjoy the ride. When everything goes well on the bus, that usually means you will be having a good day at school. God really wants us to show His lovingkindness to everyone.

I ran to the bus every morning, wondering what the new day would bring. I only lived two miles from school but for some reason, I was always the first to be picked up and the last one to get off the bus. I didn't have an assigned seat. I could sit in any seat I wanted if I behaved. The worst things that happened on the bus were yelling and throwing paper wads. Of course, the boys always liked to tease the girls. The best things were chatting with our friends, planning what we would do at recess, singing, and reading our books to each other.

We liked the high school boys and girls. They were kind to us. We also liked our bus driver, John. He liked to tease and play jokes, but he could also be strict if we broke a bus rule. At Christmas, he gave us a candy bar and at the end of the year an ice cream cone. Yum!

Riding the bus is a privilege. I hope you will have many fun memories of your trips to school. If you are kind to everyone, it can happen for you.

1. What kind of rules do you have on your bus?

2. What excites you most about school?

3. Why is being able to ride the bus a privilege?

The Greatest Treasure

2 Corinthians 4:7
   "But we have this treasure in earthen vessels…"

It's spring! I'm ready to look for treasures outdoors in the warm sunshine. I see treasures in the flower beds. It's the beautiful tulips and daffodils getting ready to bloom and fill the yard with color. Have you ever looked for a treasure? Maybe under a rock pile or in the sand at the beach? What did you find? A jewel? An old coin? A pretty seashell? Or a toy that had been buried for a long time? We could look for the pot of gold at the end of an April rainbow. That would be quite a treasure if it were real.

One summer day, long ago, I found some pieces of glass. They were so pretty. Each piece was a dark blue and sparkled when I held them up in the sunlight. I quickly put my newfound treasure in my pocket and ran to show Mom. She told me it was just a broken bottle. What I thought was a rich treasure was not a treasure at all.

When I got a little older, I learned from the Bible I could have the greatest treasure of all by asking Jesus to come into my heart and be my Savior. Now I have a treasure that no one can take from me. I hope you have found that treasure.

1. Is it okay to have earthly treasures?

2. What do you treasure most on earth?

3. Do you have the greatest of all treasures (Jesus) in your heart?

Our Friend, Uncle Jake

Proverbs 18:24
   "A man who has friends, must himself be friendly."

Uncle Jake was not really an uncle but that's what we called him. He was a good friend. He was short, with dark hair and black eyes. He loved popping in to say 'hello'. He always made himself at home. The kitchen was his favorite place to plop down on a chair. Uncle Jake seemed lonely. He loved being with my big family. We kids were glad to see him because he always took time to talk to us.

Many times, he'd say, "Come on kids, let's go fishing." Uncle Jake showed us the best places to dig for fishing worms. As soon as the coffee can was overflowing with worms, we were ready to go. At the big gravel pit, we had to climb down a hill through dirt and grass to get to the 'beach'. It wasn't sandy like a real beach, just bare dirt. If it had rained recently, it would be muddy. We loved squishing the mud between our toes and then putting our feet in the water to wash them off. Uncle Jake helped us get our 'bamboo' poles ready. We had to put the bait on ourselves. Yuk! We'd catch baby bluegills and small catfish. We never kept them, just threw them back to catch again. Soon the cows were mooing and moving toward the barn to be milked. Uncle Jake helped drive them up to the barn area and then said he had to leave. We were sad but knew he would come back another day to fish. Uncle Jake was a good friend.

1. Do you have a special friend?

2. What do you do to make friends?

3. Have you made Jesus your friend?

The Night the Firemen Came

Joshua 1:5b
   I will not leave you nor forsake you."

The snow kept coming down. It was beautiful and getting deeper around the house and down the lane. Dad came in from checking the animals and he had snow in his ears. We ate supper and continued to watch the snow. We kids were excited, making it hard to go to sleep. We wanted to stay up and watch the snow.

"Get up, kids! Get up! Hurry! Hurry!" Mom yelled.

"The house is on fire!" We smelled the smoke and ran pell-mell down the stairway, not thinking to grab our clothes. We were running for safety in our pajamas!

It was two o'clock in the morning. Dad ran out of the house in his long underwear, coat, hat, and boots. We had just moved into our house and didn't have a phone yet. Wading through snow drifts, down the long lane to the neighbors, he asked them to please call the fire department. The firemen came and quickly put out the fire. A fireplace mantel had broken loose from the wall and fell over against the wood stove causing the fire. The firemen did a good job. We were all safe.

The fire truck cleared the snow enough for us to get down the lane and over to the neighbor's house. Mrs. Cobb fixed us a wonderful breakfast of pancakes, eggs, and toast. We had a great time eating breakfast at the neighbors in our pajamas. I'm so glad God watched over us and kept us safe.

1. Do you know the rules when there is a fire?

2. Has your family planned a safe place for everyone to meet?

3. Talk about the things you and your family can do to be safe in case of fire.

Bearing Good Fruit

John 15:16

"You did not choose Me, but I chose you and appointed you that you should go and bear fruit..."

Do you have a favorite fruit? Is it apples, oranges, grapes, peaches, or something different? Maybe you like blackberries, strawberries, or raspberries best. God has given us so many to choose from. And when they are ripe, they just melt in our mouth. When the berries first ripen on the trees and bushes, my sisters and I had to hurry and get them picked before the birds gobbled them up. They always got their share though. Mom would freeze some, but she would also make pies and cobblers. Yum!

When Jesus said He chose us to "bear fruit,' He wasn't talking about the fruit we eat. He wanted us to share His 'heavenly fruit' which is: love, kindness, joy, gentleness, peace, patience, and goodness. That's the kind of fruit that helps people feel happy.

1. Where do blackberries and raspberries grow?

2. How about peaches and apples? Where will you find them?

3. Can you name a very important vitamin we get by eating fruit?

He Prepares a Place

John 14:2

Jesus said, "I go to prepare a place for you…"

The school year is over. No more getting up early to catch the bus. No more wondering if homework is all done. No more studying for tests. Summer is here! My sisters and I hurry to the corncrib to see if all the corn is gone. The hogs had eaten almost all of their 'corn on the cob.' We sweep out all the dirt and leftover corn kernels. We are preparing the corncrib to be our playhouse for summer fun. We bring out all our toys. We want to make it like a little home. Mom gives us an old bedspread.

We hang it up to hide the corn that is still in the end of the corncrib. All is finally ready, and we can hardly wait till our friends and cousins come to play. We have prepared a great place to play games and have fun during the summer months. It is our own place where we can play and do lots of pretending.

Jesus has prepared a beautiful place in heaven for us someday. It will not be just for the summer but for eternity. That means forever. He wants each of us to love Him and receive Him as our Savior so we can live with Him someday in the place He has prepared for us.

1. What have you done to prepare for a great summer?

2. Do you remember to thank those who have prepared things for you?

3. Draw a picture of the Cross to remind you of Jesus.

Be My Valentine

1 John 4:8b
"...For God is love."

I'm working on my valentine cards. Do you have your valentines ready to take to school? I remember how much fun it was to open those valentines and see who sent them. Some valentines today have suckers and candy. Wow! Don't forget to give one to Mom and Dad and your grandparents. They're not too old to get excited about how much you love them. Tell them often.

Love! That's what it's all about. Sharing your love with friends and family and even your pets. And also showing others you care when they are sad. Someone once said that love makes the world go around. I believe that is true when you know that love comes from God. The Bible tells us God is love and we can love because God first loved us. (1st John 4:19) He makes our world go around when we feel that 'warm inside happy feeling' as we share our love with others. I hope you have a loving, happy Valentine's Day.

1. What might you do to show your love today?

2. How would you feel if you didn't get a Valentine from your friend?

3. Design your own special Valentines. Have fun.

A New Thing

Isaiah 43:19
"Behold, I will do a new thing..."

God was getting ready to do a new thing in my life and it was exciting. We were going to move. I was in third grade. I would be leaving all my friends and I didn't like that. And the school would be much bigger. Instead of three grades in one room, the teacher would have only one grade. I would now have twenty classmates instead of seven. What a change for my sisters and me!

Everything was different when I arrived. It took me awhile to get used to my new teacher and to remember the names of all my classmates. The school had a top floor, a main floor, and a basement. It also had a big gym. I made sure I stayed with my class and my teacher. I didn't want to get lost in this new, big school that I now attended.

I'm glad God is always with us when we move into new places. You might just be moving to a different house. Or maybe you've lived in a small town and now your family is moving to a much bigger town. Instead of feeling sad, try thinking of all the good things that can happen as you get used to your new place, wherever it might be.

1.   Have you had to move and leave your friends?

2.   How did you feel on the first day in your new school?

3.   Did you feel lost and a little bit afraid?

Chores on the Farm

Psalm 100:4b
"Be thankful to Him and bless His name."

Sometimes we all have to do things we don't like to do. Living on a farm, there were always a lot of chores to be done. My sisters and I were six years old when we had to start doing our share of the work. Some chores weren't that much fun, but they had to be done. We didn't like scooping out the chicken house, but it had to be nice and clean for the new baby chicks. Then there was cleaning out the cow barn; washing it down with the hose. We must have smelled pretty bad when that job was done! Yuck!

Pulling gypsum weeds in the pig lot was a really smelly job in the hot summer months. Pulling weeds out of the vegetable garden wasn't quite so bad but we would rather have been reading a good book or playing with our dolls.

We didn't have running water in the house. We had to pump the water we needed. In winter, we'd wrap up in heavy coats and help carry wood in for the wood stove. Even with all the chores we had as young girls, we still had plenty of time to play and enjoy our growing up years.

Whenever you have to help with something, just thank God that you are well and healthy and can do what you are asked to do. That makes your work go much faster. Honest, it really does.

1.   What do you do at home to help?

2.   What do you do at school to help?

3.   Get up and move! Don't be lazy! Work can be fun if you have a good attitude.

My Old Shoes Kept Me Home

1 Samuel 16:7b
"...For man looks at the outward appearance, but the Lord looks at the heart."

School had just started. Third grade was going to be a good year. All my friends were in my class. One of my friends was having a birthday party on a Friday evening. I took my invitation home. I wanted to go but I knew I couldn't. Everyone would be dressed in their very best. I had a nice dress to wear but my shoes had holes in them.

They looked awful. At school, I could hide them under my desk. Mom had told me I would get new school shoes in a couple weeks when they sent the beef cattle to market. That was okay but I was too ashamed of my shoes to go to the party. All my friends begged me to be there. They couldn't understand why I didn't want to go and be a part of the fun.

God is like that. He doesn't understand why we stay home from church and worry so much about how our shoes, our clothes, or our hair looks. He must wonder why we think we have to act and dress like everyone else. God doesn't look at the outside of a person. He looks at their heart. He wants to fill our hearts with His love.

He wants each one of us to love Him more than clothes and shoes and all the 'stuff' we think we have to have. Ask God to help you look more at the hearts of the boys and girls in your class and show them His love.

1.   Do you get upset about what you are going to wear to school?

2.   How can we be more like God and look at the heart of our friends?

3.   Tell someone today how nice they look.

Skating in the Ballroom

Proverbs 14:12
"There is a way that seems right…"

Upstairs in our house was a huge room that was closed off in the winter. This room had been built for a ballroom. That's a place where ladies and gentlemen dress in their very best and dance to the music of a small orchestra. My sisters and I had a better idea. We decided to put on our roller skates and make this room our roller rink.

Snowflakes were swirling around the corners of the house. Brrr! We knew it was too cold to play outdoors. Our new plan seemed like a very good idea to us. When Mom came in from helping at the barn and heard all the noise and racket of our skates, she flew up the stairs. Our 'fun day' was over. She did not approve at all of what we had decided to do. We didn't think about how the skates might tear up the floor. Mom taught us a lesson that day to think before we act. What may seem right could be harmful.

I'm sure Jesus wants us to do the same, to think about what might happen first, then what we do will be pleasing to Him.

1. Can you think of something you have done that seemed right but was really dangerous?

2. What kind of fun things do you do in winter when you have to stay inside?

3. Is winter your favorite season? What do you like best about it?

Summertime Play

Psalm 74: 16b, 17b

"You have prepared the light and the sun...You have made summer..."

Summertime couldn't come soon enough when I was a kid. There were so many fun things to do even though we didn't have a TV or video games, or a cell phone. My sisters and I would hurry to get our chores done so we would have more time to play. Playing in the maple tree that sat on a hill in the front yard was a favorite thing to do. We would climb to the lowest branch that would hold us, scoot out a little way and hang upside down swinging back and forth.

The barn lot was the perfect place to play Kickball or Kick the Can. When they built the big brick house we lived in; the bricks were made right there in one of the fields close to the house. Many days we would play like we were building a house out of the leftover bricks. Of course, there was always a new batch of baby kittens to play with when they were old enough.

When summer turned really hot, we filled the horse tank with water and that was our swimming pool. It wasn't very big for three of us, but we were

47

happy just playing in the cold water. When it rained, we played board games, dressed up in Mom's old shoes and dresses, or just read a good book.

1. Are you glad God made summer? Can you share why you are glad?

2. Do you ever stop and listen to the birds singing and talking to each other?

3. What is the most fun thing you like to do in summer?

Cows

Genesis 2:20

"So, Adam gave names to all cattle, to the birds of the air, and to every beast of the field."

I'm not sure what names Adam gave the cattle at the time of creation in the Bible, but we gave our cows names like; Big Red, Bossy, Slick, and Princess. We had so many cows on the farm, it was hard to remember them all, but they knew their names. When it was milking time on the farm, the cows knew exactly which stall was theirs in the barn.

My sisters and I had to make sure the cows had plenty of hay to eat while they were being milked. That helped the cows to stand still. I loved the cows. They were gentle and had pretty eyes. They wouldn't hurt you unless you tried to hurt their baby calves. Of course, they were big animals, so we had to stay out of their way. There are cows all over the world. God knew we would need the cows so we would have milk to drink, milk for ice cream, milk for all kinds of cheeses, milk for baking cakes and cookies and cornbread, milk for yogurt, and so many more good things. He is a good God.

1. Have you been around cows on the farm?

2. Can you name other foods that we get from the cow?

3. Do you know how the milk gets from the cow to the grocery store?

My First School

Proverbs 1:5
"A wise man will hear and increase learning."

School is the place for listening and learning. My first school only had three rooms. The first and 2nd grade were in one room. The third, fourth, and fifth grades were in the middle room, and the sixth, seventh, and eighth grades were in the biggest room.

We had a coat room where we hung our coats and put our lunches on a shelf. Our boots were to be placed neatly under where our coats were hanging. I was timid and shy but soon became used to the big second graders on the other side of the room. First grade started by learning to write cursive. While the teacher taught us the cursive letters, the second graders were reading. Then she taught their writing lesson while we practiced our cursive letters. She would go back and forth through the day teaching math and reading as well. We would have art projects often and some days we would learn new songs. I loved singing. P.E. was always our recess time.

Third, fourth, and fifth grades were in the middle room. When I was in third grade I listened and learned a lot just watching the teacher as she taught

51

the other classes their lessons. I liked everything about being at school.

1.   Have you ever had to go to a new school?

2.   What do you like best about school?

3.   Do you like to learn about new things?

My Special Aunt

John 13:34
"A new commandment I give to you, that you love one another as I have loved you."

Do you have someone in your family that makes you feel special? Someone who lets you know you are loved? My Aunt Lula was like that. She was always glad to see me.

The summer I was nine years old, my sister and I got to spend three weeks at her house. What an exciting time we had. Aunt Lula baked cookies with us, taught us to ride a bike, sewed play clothes for us, and walked us to the park on sunny days.

Her husband worked for the railroad. He was in charge of the roundhouse, making sure the trains were all on the right tracks. He had a lot of stories to tell us about the trains and the people who rode them.

My aunt loved to work in her flowers, but her greatest love was telling stories about Jesus. Every day she would tell us a different story from the Bible: how Jesus told Zacchaeus to come down from the tree, how He blessed the little children, how He walked on water, how He healed the sick, and how He fed five thousand people with just five loaves of bread and two fish. Wow! So many wonderful stories of how Jesus showed His love for people.

1. Name someone who makes you feel special.

2. Why is it important that we love one another?

3. What are some stories that you have learned from reading your Bible?

Learning to Work

John 9:4
*I must work the works of Him who sent Me while it is
day..."*

Jesus knew how important it was to do the work God
had for Him to do. You may think you are too little
to work, but even when we are young, we can be good
workers.

Granny was 4 years old when my Mom pulled a
chair up to the sink and began to teach me how to
wash the dishes. I couldn't wash the knives and the
big pots and pans. And I had to be very careful not to
break anything. I'm sure Mom had to remind me not
to play in the water but to wash the dishes.

I also learned to sweep the back porch, clean my
room, and pick up my toys. There was always a lot to
do but Mom didn't make me work all the time. She
made sure I had time to play.

God wants us to learn to be good workers.
Moms and Dads work hard, and they sometimes need
extra help. It's also important for us to do our very
best work, always.

Work helps us to grow strong. Work is good for us. And another good thing; we never get bored. It's the right thing to do.

1. Name 5 ways that show you are a good worker like Jesus.

2. Why is it so important to learn how to do new things?

3. If you see someone drop all their books and papers, what do you do?

Our Pet Billy Goat

Jeremiah 33:3
"Call to Me and I will answer you, and show you great and mighty things, which you do not know."

I was ten years old the day Dad told us something special was coming to our house. My sisters and I could hardly sleep that night wondering what this special thing would be. We kept guessing but we never came up with the right answer.

That something special was a Billy Goat! Was he ever cute! He was all brown with white ears and a white tail. He had big black eyes that looked at us like he knew everything we were saying. He loved to prance around and act tough.

Our older brother made a cart so Billy could take us rides. We had fun riding around the barn lot and down the lane. There was one problem with Billy, though. When we got halfway down the lane, Billy decided he was hungry. He headed for the ditch and started eating anything he could find. We screamed and yelled at him, but he ignored us. We started laughing at him. But he just turned around and looked at us and kept right on chewing and eating. What a funny pet! Billy Goat didn't always listen to us.

But Jesus is not like that. Jesus listens when we call His name. In our scripture verse today, He tells us to call to Him and He will answer. When you are hurting or having a problem, He will be listening. Jesus always answers when you call.

1.   Some say Jeremiah 33:3 is God's telephone number. Why is that?

2.   Do you think Billy the Goat made a good pet? In what way?

3.   Draw a picture of what you think Billy and the cart looked like.

Billy Goat Gets Away

Genesis 1:25

God made the beast (animals)...according to its kind."

Billy Goat was getting used to his new home on our friend's farm. He was doing a good job keeping the weeds eaten in the orchard. But one day something changed. Even though he liked all the other animals, Billy began looking around and decided he would go exploring.

He took a flying leap and over the fence he went. We found him on our front porch. We were excited to see him, but knew we had to take him back. The next day, he was back again.

"That goat is just lonely for other goats like him," said the farmer. He picked him up and let him ride in his truck to the goat farm a few miles away. They had black goats, gray goats, white goats, and speckled goats. Some had horns, some had long ears, and some had short ears. They were all different but as soon as Billy saw all the different goats, he began to holler at them in goat language. He was happy. As far as I know, he never jumped the fence again.

Like Billy and the goats, there are all different kinds of people. We are different

colors. We are different sizes. We like to do different activities. We like different foods.

But God wants us to love each other, no matter how different we may be.

1. Why did Billy keep coming back?

2. What made Billy stop jumping the fence?

3. What tells you Billy was finally happy?

Reading Takes You Places

1 Timothy 4:13-14a
"Till I come, give attention to reading...Do not neglect the gift that is in you..."

Granny has lived a long time and I have had an exciting life, but I've never flown a kite, skydived from an airplane, learned how to swim, or sailed on an ocean liner. I've never explored a cave, drove a motorcycle, or went deep-sea fishing. I have never para-sailed over the ocean, drove a semi, or traveled to distant lands. What's more, I haven't jumped on a trampoline, rode a ten-speed bike, climbed a mountain, or won a gold medal at the Olympics.

I've never been involved in any of these happenings in person, but by reading books, magazines, and newspapers about these events, I feel the excitement one must have when they take part in any of them.

Reading can take you places you have never been and show you sights you have never seen. Reading can make you laugh. Sometimes the stories are sad and make you cry. Reading can make you feel like flying to the top of a mountain.

Reading can be your eye to see the world. Life is never boring when you take time to read. In the Bible, the greatest book of all, Paul tells us to be sure to give attention to reading. Of all God's creations, only we humans have this gift: the ability to read and understand.

1. What kind of books do you like to read?

2. Do you try to read something every day? Especially in the summer?

3. Try writing your own book about an activity where you have been a part

Callie, The Cat

2 Chronicles 16:9
> *"For the eyes of the Lord run to and fro throughout the whole earth, to show Himself strong on behalf of those whose heart is loyal to Him."*

Callie was a very special cat. She just showed up on our doorstep one morning wanting to be fed. Her eyes looked at us longingly, wondering if she could stay. Of course, we all loved and petted her. She wasn't the most beautiful cat, but she was smart. All the love we gave her made her decide to make her home with us. Even our dog, who normally didn't like cats, made friends with her. My sisters and I dressed Callie in doll clothes and pushed her in the doll stroller. She'd play for a while with us and then she'd hop out and run and hide. Dressing up in clothes was just not what Callie liked to do. She always came back later to see what we were doing.

Every day when Callie heard the bus bringing us home from school, she would run from the barn to the back step. She wanted to be the first one to greet us. I could tell that she missed us. I would sweep her up in my arms and nuzzle her fur. She smelled just like new mown hay and fresh air. Callie stayed with us for over a year and then all at once she was gone. We looked everywhere on the farm but no Callie. We looked up and down the road to make sure a car had not hit her. We could not find one trace of our precious, lovable cat. Where could she have gone?

Just as we looked everywhere for Callie, the Bible says that God's eyes are always looking for us. He wants us to stay close to Him and follow His ways.

1. What are some funny things that cats do? How about your cat?

2. Where do you think Callie could have gone?

3. Draw a picture of your cat or whatever pet you have.

Callie Comes Home

Luke 15:20b

"...his father saw him and had compassion and ran and fell on his neck and kissed him."

Callie, where could she be? She was still missing, and snow would soon be falling. Callie liked sleeping on the hay in the warm barn. Did someone take her? Did she get hit by a big truck? Did a coyote catch her as she hunted in the night? We didn't know. We only knew how much we missed Callie and hoped she was okay.

The months went by and still no trace of Callie. Then one spring day while in the garden, we heard a soft "meow." We couldn't see anything but then we saw the tip of a tail through the tall grass. "It's Callie!" We screamed. She came walking up to us as if she had never been gone. She was thin and needed a good brushing. We petted her and didn't want to ever let her go.

"She's hungry," Mom said. "Let's get her some food." After feeding her, she looked at us and purred as if to say, "I'm so glad to be home." Callie lived with us for many years, but we never knew where she had been those months she was gone.

The Bible tells about a young man who left his home. His father missed him very much. When the young man decided how much he missed his family, he returned. His father was excited and ran and kissed his son. God is like that. When we go away from Him and forget to pray or go to church, He is sad and misses us. God is always excited when we talk to Him and let Him know how much we love Him, because He loves us.

1. Wouldn't it be nice if Callie could share where she had been?

2. What do you think she would tell us?

3. Do you think her family prayed for her?

Cell Phones Do Many Things

Proverbs 25: 2
  "It is the glory of God to conceal a matter..."

I have this little gadget that will take pictures. I can send and receive messages from people, and I can talk to anyone, anywhere in the United States. It is small enough to carry in my pocket or on my belt. Have you guessed what my little gadget is? "A cell phone? Yeah, you are right!"

How different the cell phone is. When Granny was your age, our phone was a funny looking box made of wood that hung on the wall. It had two bells at the top that rang when someone called. A black mouthpiece was right in the middle that we talked into, much like a microphone. There was a little shelf at the bottom of the box in case I wanted to take a message.

The receiver was on the side of the box. I held the receiver to my ear. If I wanted to call someone, there was a little handle on the other side of the box that I turned. If you wanted to call me; my number was 28F12. If you wanted to speak with the operator you would turn the handle only one time. In those days, no one could imagine the wonderful cell phones we have today and all they can do. It was a hidden idea that no one had discovered yet.

The Bible is like that. It has many hidden truths for you to discover. As you are growing up and studying God's Word, He will show you many of these hidden truths. It is up to us to search for all that God has hidden in His Word.

1. How is the cell phone different than the phone Granny had?

2. Are cell phones just for playing games?

3. Name 3 reasons you would need a cell phone.

Not My Best Day

Psalm 121:2

"My help comes from the Lord, who made heaven and earth."

I knew when I woke up early and felt dizzy, this wasn't going to be my best day. My tummy hurt. None of the food Mom was making for breakfast smelled good. I wanted to stay under the covers and keep warm. But all I could think about was the special day at school. It was the day of the Christmas party. We were to bring our gifts. I had made a special gift for my teacher and one for the friend whose name I had drawn. If I didn't go, they wouldn't have a gift. Why did I have to get sick today? I cried but Mom told me there would be other Christmas parties. And Dad said he would take my gifts to the school.

We don't know why things happen as they do but we know God's word tells us He is always helping us through those times when we are sad or not feeling our best. That's a good thing to know and remember.

1. Have you ever missed a special day at school? How did you feel?

2. Who takes care of you when you are sick?

3. What does God mean when He says He will never leave us? How can that be?

Our Christmas Visitor

Galatians 5:13b
"...*but through love, serve one another.*"

The teachers were trying to keep us quiet. But excitement filled the air. It was the last day before Christmas break and all the elementary students and teachers were walking the two blocks to the theater in our small town to see the movie 'Bambi.'

Getting to see this movie was the teacher's gift to all the students. As we stood in line at the theater, I saw a serviceman. He looked so handsome in his uniform. He walked over by us. He didn't see me, but I recognized him. I told my friends he was my brother. They laughed and said I was making it up. I thought maybe I was mistaken because it had been almost three years since he left to serve in the Coast Guard.

The teachers began moving us along to see the movie. I enjoyed watching *Bambi* and forgot all about the serviceman. But when I got home, what a surprise waited for me. The handsome man WAS my brother. He picked me up and spun me around. He was surprised that I had seen him at the theater. My brother had only ten days to be with us. He was serving our country and had to report back to his ship. It was good to see him and hear about all the places he had been. He was our Christmas visitor that year.

1. Do you have someone in your family who is serving in the military?

2. Did they serve on a ship or on a plane? Or were they serving on the ground?

3. Why does our country need the military?

Your Favorite Toy

James 1:17a
"Every good gift and every perfect gift is from above, and comes down from the Father of lights...."

What was the favorite toy you received for Christmas last year? Was it a train, a new video, a doll, or a stuffed animal? Where are they now? If that toy could talk, it might tell you how much fun the two of you had together; how you took the toy everywhere you went, shared it with your friends, and maybe even slept with it.

But then as the days and weeks went by it would tell of how you lost interest in your favorite Christmas toy. You left it on the floor to be stepped on or threw it in the toy box underneath everything else, or even left it outside to be rained on or carried away by the neighbor's dog. Your favorite toy might tell you, "It's not too late for you to pick me up and dust me off and put me someplace special, so I can be with you when you are older." A friend of mine, who now has grandchildren, still has two dolls she got for Christmas when she was just a little girl.

Take good care of your toys and gifts you get at Christmas and all through the year. They each were

73

given in love by someone special who cares for you. God cares so much for you and me, He gave us the greatest gift of all, his Son, Jesus.

1. Do you have a special place for your toys?

2. What should we say to people who give us presents/gifts?

3. What do we say to God for His Son, Jesus?

Why Christmas Is Special

Matthew 1:21
   "And she will bring forth a Son, and you shall call His name Jesus, for He will save His people from their sins."

Three cheers for Christmas! What makes Christmas so special for you? Could it be the extra candy and goodies or is it the delightful Christmas movies? Maybe it's the gifts and toys, you are hoping to get. These are certainly a part of making Christmas fun and exciting. But a baby boy born in Bethlehem in Judea over 2000 years ago is what really makes the holiday we call Christmas so very, very special.

His mother, Mary, and stepfather, Joseph, did not get to name this baby. His Heavenly Father, God, said His name would be Jesus, because he would save His people from their sins.

Did you know Jesus brought many gifts with Him when He came? Gifts of love, joy, peace, and hope. These are gifts that make Christmas a Holy Holiday, different from any other. The greatest is that Jesus keeps on giving. You can find many more gifts as you read the Bible. I hope you have a joy filled Christmas this year.

1. How does your family celebrate Christmas?

2. What makes it so special to you?

3. Can you find 3 more gifts that Jesus has given to us.

God's Great Goodness

Psalm 31:19
"Oh, how great is Your goodness..."

Granny was nine years old and there was a war going on across the ocean. Many Americans were fighting to protect our country. Our teacher told us how we could help by collecting milkweed pods. These were found growing along the roads, in the fields, and in the woods. Caterpillars love to eat the leaves of this plant before they go into their cocoon.

The pod of the milkweed has a silky fiber inside that was placed in material to make life jackets. These were needed by the soldiers and sailors on ships and in airplanes, in case they had to bail out (jump) into the ocean. Our entire school collected many burlap bags full of these milkweed pods.

We also saved newspaper, tinfoil, and tin cans. These were used in several ways to help those who were serving in the Army, Navy, Marines, and Coast Guard. By doing our part we were showing the goodness of God to others.

1. What do you do to help your country? Or your town?

2. Do you recycle plastic, glass, and metal?

3. What other ways can you show God's goodness?

Planting Cornfield Beans

Isaiah 28:21b
"That He may do His work, His awesome work…"

The corn is growing? It's about three inches high. I can still hear Dad say, "Come on, kids. It's time to plant the cornfield beans." We groaned. We had a lot of playing we wanted to do. Planting cornfield beans was work. Dad made us a pole from a shortened broomstick. We punched a hole in the dirt beside each corn plant and put two bean seeds in the hole. As the corn grew the bean plant would vine around the corn stalk. Sometimes we tried to put more than two beans in the hole, so we'd get done sooner. But Dad always seemed to know.

In the fall, we picked the dry beans that hung on the corn stalk. That was a hot, scratchy job. After picking the beans, the fun began. We put the dried beans, into gunny sacks, made of burlap. Then we jumped up and down on them (like you do on the trampoline) until all the beans were out of their pods. Of course, there was a lot of chaff, gunky stuff, that had to be gotten out of the beans. We each took two pans and poured the beans back and forth and let the wind blow the chaff away. Pouring the beans to get rid of the chaff is called 'winnowing.' They had to do this with the wheat back in Jesus' day. Chaff is a lot like sin, not good. We don't want it in our lives. And we didn't want that old chaff in our beans either. They always tasted so good when Mom cooked them with ham and made cornbread. Yum!

1. This Bible verse says God does awesome work. What do you think He does?

2. What kind of work do you do?

3. Make a list of the things you do to help Mom and Dad.

Towser and the Cows

Genesis 2:19
  "Out of the ground, the Lord God formed every beast of the field..."

The cows on the farm were led to the pasture after they were milked in the early morning. By evening time, they would need to be milked again. In the summertime, we would take our dog, Towser, and head back to the field where the cows were. Towser, being a good farm dog, knew just what to do. He would run around them barking as we started calling out to them. Sometimes we would say the name of the cows we knew, but mostly we called them the way Dad called them: "Sulk, cow, Sulk, cow."

They seemed to understand this meant they were going to get food and be milked. They would lift their head, look at us as if to say, "What do you want?" Then they would walk to the path that led to the barn. Towser kept them in a straight line. The cows plodded along, swishing their tails back and forth, and mooing to their hearts content.

God made the cow to be a gentle animal. Sometimes though they have bad days just like you and me. They don't always act as gentle as God created them to be. On those days, we didn't get too close to them.

1. Towser was a worker dog. How do you know that from the story?

2. The cows were out in the field. How do you think the cows knew about the path to the barn?

3. Why do you think the cows were mooing?

Always Tell the Truth

Exodus 20:16
"You shall not bear false witness (lie) against your neighbor (a friend)."

Have you ever gotten into trouble for doing something wrong? It happened to me when I was six years old. It was big trouble for me because I lied. It was about something really important.

It was a winter evening, not yet dark, but a cold winter wind was blowing. My Dad had to get the cows milked and he asked me to feed the chickens. We depended on the chickens for eggs and they needed to be fed every day especially when it was cold.

When I got to the chicken house, I saw there was a little bit of feed in their feeders. I decided that was good enough. I ran back to the house where it was warm and cozy.

Dad came in later and asked me if I fed the chickens. I said, "Yes." He knew I hadn't been at the chicken house long enough to do the job right. He knew I lied, and I got one of the hardest spankings of my life. I didn't like that spanking, but I know now that God didn't want me to grow up to be a person who never told the truth. God makes it very plain in the Bible that we are not to lie. Jesus calls the devil the Father of Lies. He might tell you it's okay to lie, but don't let him trick you. Always tell the truth.

1. Why is it important to always tell the truth?

2. Can someone be hurt if we lie?

3. What did God want Granny to be?

The Button Box

Acts 9:39b

"And all the widows stood by him weeping, showing the tunics and garments which Dorcas had made while she was with them."

Like Dorcas in our scripture verse, my mom loved to sew. She made almost all our clothes. She would sew late into the night so we would have a new outfit to wear for a special occasion. She sewed dresses, blouses, skirts, coats, and even long pants for us to wear in snowy weather.

When I was young, we wore our best clothes to school and church. When we got home, we changed into everyday play clothes. As our clothes wore out, we put them in the ragbag to be made into rugs or comforters or quilts. But first we had to take all the buttons off and save them in a tin box.

That tin box was a lot of fun to play with on a winter day. It was full of every shape, size, and color of button. We would play with them for hours building imaginary roads. Then we would sort them by color and size. We used those buttons to learn how to count and how to add and subtract. We never got tired of playing with that tin box of buttons. The lady in our Bible verse, Dorcas, made many kinds of clothing for the people in the town of Joppa where she lived. She was helping others just as Jesus tells us to do.

1. Do you have a button box?

2. Have you ever thought about who sewed your clothes?

3. Try to sew something. You may like to sew

Swimming at the Big Pool

Exodus 14:13

"And Moses said to the people, "Do not be afraid. Stand still and see the salvation of the Lord…"

Summer was a busy time on the farm. We didn't get to go to the big pool to swim very often. But we did have a special place we would go when we had some free time. I never learned how to swim but I loved splashing and playing in the water. This pool had a huge slide, at least it seemed big to me. Dad said if I wanted to slide down, he would catch me so I wouldn't go under the water. When I got to the top, I saw Dad waiting in the water, so I started down. The slide was slick, and I went zooming down. I was going so fast Dad couldn't catch me. I went under and came up sputtering and very scared.

Like me, the people in Moses' day were afraid of the water. The Red Sea looked huge and very frightening to them. But Moses explained that God would be there watching them, and they would be safe.

1. Have you learned how to swim?

2. Why is it important to be with someone when you are in the water?

3. How does God help you when you are afraid?

Elsie, The Borden Cow

Hebrews 13:16a
"But do not forget to do good and to share..."

Elsie, the Borden Cow, is not a real cow. She was invented back in 1936 to advertise for the Borden Milk Company. Growing up, I had an Elsie Board Game. Elsie and her husband, Elmer, had a son whose was named Beauregard. That was her little family and there were always cute pictures of them on the Borden products. They were a big part of the toys and commercials. Elsie's picture was on lunch boxes, cookie jars, and many other collectibles. There were even dolls made to look like Elsie. Her toys were very popular just like your favorite toys today.

A cow that looked like Elsie was always at the State Fair. She would be dressed in her finest; a daisy chain around her neck and a red ribbon on her tail. The children petted her on the nose. She liked all that attention.

Have you thanked God for all the special toys you have? There are many boys and girls in the world and maybe in your own community, who do not have many toys. If you have toys you have outgrown or do not play with, this might be a good time to wash them and share with somebody who is longing for a new and different toy. I think Jesus would like that.

1. Do you have a special toy that you see on lunchboxes?

2. Why would God tell us in the Bible to "do good and share?"

3. Can you name some fathers in the Bible?

Filling the Coal Bucket

1 Corinthians 10:31b
   "...whatever you do, do all to the glory of God."

We climbed out from under the covers and began to shake and shiver. It was the month of February and the cold winds of winter found every little crack in the windowsill and blew right through that crack to make us wish we didn't have to get out from under the covers. We hurried down the stairs in our flannel pajamas to warm ourselves beside the pot-bellied stove in the kitchen. Dad always had a hot fire going for us.

After school, it was our job to fill the coal buckets. The only problem; the coal room was in the basement. We didn't like going down to that cold, damp place where spiders scampered up the walls and sometimes a mouse skittered across our path. My sisters and I went together because it was too scary to go alone. Besides, it was hard work picking up those big chunks of coal.

This was one chore we had to get done. Dad had told us without the coal, he could not build the fire for us to huddle close to on cold mornings. Dad had to milk twenty cows; morning and evening and he needed us to do our part. Sometimes the chores we have to do are not much fun, but they are very important.

Remember God tells us to do (our chores) for His glory. Singing songs to God while I worked always helped me get done much quicker.

1.   What are some chores you do every day?

2.   Do you have a good attitude about your work?

3.   Have you ever noticed all the little chores Mom and Dad do for you?

Flying High

Psalm 55:6
"Oh, that I had wings like a dove! I would fly away and be at rest."

King David, in this Psalm, thought it would be nice to have wings and be able to fly somewhere to rest. He didn't know that many, many years later, people would be flying in planes that had wings.

When I was ten years old, my Uncle Clifton decided to take a few of us in his small plane. I was excited. After Uncle buckled us in, he climbed into the cockpit and revved the motor. The plane began moving down the runway. The runway was a cow pasture. Soon the plane began lifting into the air. What a thrill to look down and see the fields and all the different colors. They looked like a big patchwork quilt. The barns and houses and animals all seemed so small. My family looked like little people as they waved to us.

After circling a few times, Uncle Clifton began to bring the plane down. The cows were in the way, so he had to buzz them. He had to fly really close to the cows to scare them off the runway so we could land. I don't think the cows liked the noisy airplane using their field for landing space.

God didn't give us wings but He did give some people the gift of wisdom to invent the flying machines. Some people say they feel closer to God when they are flying high in the sky.

1. What would we do without the airplanes?

2. How many ways do people use the small planes? The jets?

3. Do you think it is true that we can feel closer to God in an airplane?

Going to the Movies (The Free Show)

Genesis 1:16
"Then God made two great lights, the greater light to rule the day and the lesser light to rule the night. He made the stars also."

I was six years old and we were going to the free show. The neighbor children wanted to go with us, so we packed extra blankets and plenty of popcorn and began piling in the car. But the car wouldn't hold all of us. Some of us had to ride in the trunk. We only had to go about two miles. Dad left the trunk lid up so we could see out. He didn't drive very fast because it was a gravel road. He knew we would get dust in our eyes and hair.

We went to the grocery store in town. It was a 2-story, tall, white building. The side of the building made a perfect movie screen. We spread our blankets on the cool grass and waited till it was dark enough to see the movie. It was in black and white and usually was a western or a comedy show that made us laugh. Sometimes it was a love story the moms and dads liked. We kids either fell asleep or slipped off to play with others in the nearby church yard.

Riding home in the trunk we got to see more pictures in the sky. The moon, the stars, the Milky Way, the Big and Little Dipper, and even a falling star now and then. We made a wish when we saw a star fall from the sky. We always wondered where it would land. I'm glad God made the night as beautiful as the day.

When you are out walking at night, take time to look up at the sky and see all God has created for us.

1. Why did God make the sun, moon, and stars?

2. Have you ever wished on a falling star?

3. How were those free shows different than the movies you see?

Gathering the Eggs

Psalm 51:8a

"Make me hear joy and gladness..."

One of my after-school jobs was gathering the eggs. Mom made a basket lined with soft material for the eggs. I had to be careful not to crack the eggs when I put them in the basket. It was always a surprise to see how many eggs were in each nest. But it wasn't fun when the hens got feisty. They had been those sweet little baby chicks, fluffy and soft. Now they had grown into big hens with an attitude.

I reached into the nest and the eggs felt warm. Of course, the hens wanted to protect their eggs. They could get really sassy. They'd ruffle their feathers, spread their wings, and begin to squawk loudly. The minute I got my hand close, the hens started pecking as hard as they could. That hurt, but I knew I had to get all the eggs.

The next day after school I had the same job to do all over again. Some of the hens were nice if you talked softly to them. But there were always a few that didn't want to give up and let me have their eggs.

Sometimes we are like those hens. We don't want to give up and do what is right. We get up with a bad attitude and grumpy as a growly bear. And we start picking at each other instead of being joyful and glad. God tells us very plainly He wants to hear joy and gladness in our lives. I hope you will remember not to be like those feisty hens with a bad attitude.

1.   Do you like eggs with toast and bacon for breakfast?

2.   Why do you think the hens didn't want me to get their eggs?

3.   Even though you may not live on a farm, what is your job after school?

George, The Rooster

Proverbs 16:18
 "Pride goes before…a fall."

George thought he was big stuff. He was a huge rooster that ran around in our orchard with all the other chickens. He strutted and pranced everywhere letting all who came into the orchard know he was boss. If he could have worn a T-shirt, it would probably have said 'Roosters Rule.' He chased the hens away from the feeders. He wanted it for himself. He acted very selfish and prideful. When it came time for me to gather the eggs, I opened the gate, and George looked up. He began to ruffle his feathers and lift his wings like he was going to fly. He didn't fly but he came running to keep me out of the orchard. I had to carry a big stick to shoo him away or I wouldn't have been able to gather the eggs.

After I had gotten all the eggs in my basket and started for the gate, George just

looked at me and kept scratching in the dirt to find a big, fat, juicy worm. Yuck! I guess he was tired of being a mean, old, rooster.

I don't think God would like it if we acted like George. Do you?

1. Why do you think George was so mean? Would he make a good pet?

2. What is pride?

3. Is it okay to be proud when we work hard and do well?

My Lovable Grandad

Isaiah 46:9a

"Remember the former things of old..."

Grandad was a lovable man. His thick mop of snow-white hair was always falling down his forehead. He had a sparkle in his eyes that let you know right away; he was glad to see you. Grandad was not a very large man, but he made up for it in all the things he could do. He fixed cars, trucks, toasters, and sweepers. Anything that would no longer work. Back in Grandad's day, just because something broke you didn't throw it away, you fixed it.

Grandad had something about him that was very unusual. He had a pointy finger. It was the first finger on his right hand. No matter what he did, that finger would never bend. In the evening, we all sat around the fireplace and listened to the Lone Ranger on the radio. Grandad listened as he rocked in his favorite rocker. His pointy finger always seemed to be pointing at us. I always wondered what made his finger like that but was too shy to ask. After I grew up, I learned he had caught his finger in the gears of a threshing machine. That pointy finger is one of the many things I remember about my lovable Grandad.

Your grandparents have many stories of the fun things they did growing up. God tells us to remember those who are older and let them know how much they are loved.

1. What are some special things you remember about your grandparents?

2. Do you remember a favorite time you spent with your grandparents?

3. Can you remember some of the special places they have taken you?

Grandma Millie

1 John 4:8b
   "...for God is love."

Grandma Millie was a little overweight and walked ever so slow. We held her hands and tried to help her go faster, but she just couldn't. Of course, we didn't know what it was like to be her age. She was a happy person. Her eyes twinkled when she smiled which was most of the time.

Grandma Millie loved to visit our playhouse we had set up in the corncrib. She would tell us stories of when she was a little girl. She never seemed to tire of being a part of our playtime. She looked at our toys and told us many of her toys were homemade. Her eyes took on a faraway look as she shared about her cornstalk dolls with corn silk hair, and the shoebox that was their doll bed.

God blessed Grandma Millie with a love for children. She was kind and always had the right words when we got into arguments. She sure knew how to share God's love with us.

1. How was Grandma Millie's toys different than yours?

2. Do you have someone like Grandma Millie in your family? In your church?

3. How did Grandma Millie show God's love?

Helping on the Farm

Romans 16:1-2b

"...*Phoebe...has been a helper of many and of myself also.*"

Being a helper is so important and farmers always helped each other during haymaking time on the farm, which was in June. The hay would be cut, and it would lay on the field to dry. If there was a heavy dew on the hay, farmers would sit under the big maple tree and talk about their crops and how their cows and pigs were doing.

As soon as the hay was dry, they would head to the field with their tractors and equipment. First, the hay was raked up and then they would use a big fork to put it on the wagon and take it to the barn to be put in the haymow. The cows loved the hay when they came in to be milked. They liked it just like we like mashed potatoes and gravy.

I had lots of time to play on the farm, but I also had to be a helper. There was a lot of work to be done every day. I helped feed hay to the cows, corn to the pigs, and gather the eggs. And Mom always needed help in the house.

God wants us to be helpers; to help our Mom and Dad with all the chores that need to be done. Work helps us to grow strong.

1.   Name ways that show you are a good helper.

2.   Why is it so important to be a good helper?

3.   If your friend broke their leg, how could you help him/her?

Hot Butter Blue Beans

Revelation 3:20
"Behold, I stand at the door and knock..."

Yay, it's recess. Let's play 'Hot Butter Blue Beans'."
We were excited as we scrambled out the door onto
the cement porch of our three-room school. We were
glad to be out in the warm May sunshine.

The object of the game, as I remember it, was
very simple: We were to run all the way around the
building. If it had rained, the back side of the school
building was a huge mud hole. All that mud would
have brought joy to a pig's heart. The person who was
'It' had a switch. His or her goal was to switch as
many as they could and the ones they switched would
be on their team.

Of course, we ran as fast as our legs could carry
us. In the winter it wasn't so bad to get switched
because we had our coats and snow-pants on. But in
warm weather, we girls just had our dresses and long
socks on. Oh, that switch could sting if we got caught.
I'm sure that game would never be allowed in school
today.

I'm so glad Jesus doesn't use a switch to get us
on His team. In our scripture, we find that Jesus

107

knocks on the door of our heart and asks if He might come in. He is always polite and uses good manners. If we accept Him as our Savior, we can be on His team of believers forever and ever. I hope you have opened your heart and allowed

Jesus to come in and be your Savior.

1. What are some games you like to play at recess?

2. Does this game sound a lot like the game of "Tag?"

3. Name 5 games that you can play on the playground.

The Huckster Wagon Comes Again

Matthew 6:8b

"For your Father knows the things you have need of before you ask Him."

It's time for the Huckster Wagon again, bringing many things that are needed on the farm. When Granny was a little girl, buying groceries wasn't called shopping. It was called 'trading.' Most people didn't have a lot of one-dollar or five-dollar bills in their wallet, so they traded live chickens and eggs for the things they bought from the man who owned the Huckster.

He had big crates tied on the back of the wagon. That's where he would put the chickens. As he drove away, the chickens were not happy to be leaving their home. They were squawking and flapping their wings trying to get out. It was a funny sight to see.

The people who lived in town loved to get fresh food from the farm. They also had the Breadman and the Milkman who delivered fresh bread and fresh milk to their door every day. So much different from today.

I wouldn't want to trade our grocery stores for the Huckster Wagon but isn't it good how God made a way in those days for people to get what they needed?

1. Have you ever traded something you had with a friend for something they had?

2. Do you know what has to happen for you to have fried chicken?

3. Draw a picture of the Huckster Wagon showing the chickens on the back.

The Huckster Wagon

Philippians 4:19
    "...God shall supply all your need according to His riches in glory by Christ Jesus."

"Hurry! Hurry! The Huckster Wagon is coming." My sisters and I grabbed our pennies and headed out the back door, slamming the screen as we went. We weren't supposed to do that, but we were so excited. All the kittens scampered off the back porch to keep from getting stepped on. The Huckster Wagon only came once a week and we didn't want to miss it. The driver always came up the lane honking his horn.

    The Huckster Wagon was an old school bus that had been made into a traveling grocery and hardware store. It was always dusty and scruffy looking from traveling on the gravel roads. But it was special because it had many items that people on the farm needed. Bread, sugar, flour, nails, brooms, and shovels were some of the things on the Huckster Wagon. Mom could even buy needles and thread for her sewing projects.

    All the items were stacked on shelves neatly on both sides of the wagon. Mom could walk up and down the aisle in the middle and shop for whatever she needed.

After Mom had picked out everything she and Dad needed, we kids were allowed to climb in the Huckster Wagon and choose some candy. We could buy a lot with a couple pennies. What a treat! A lot of farmers lived far from the towns and stores. God supplied their need through the Huckster Wagon coming to their door.

1.   Do you think the Huckster Wagon was a good thing?

2.   Why do you think they had the Huckster Wagons when Granny was a little girl?

3.   What would you buy if the "Walmart Wagon" came to your house?

My Pink Satin Sash

Jeremiah 13:11

"...as the sash clings to the waist...I have caused the whole house of Judah to cling to Me, says the Lord..."

Swimming in the summer; is there anything more fun? We dive, we jump, we splash, we turn somersaults in the water. We laugh and giggle until we wear ourselves out. We come up out of the water and our bathing suit and hair clings tight to our skin until we grab a towel and dry off.

Makes me think of my Aunt who loved to make clothes for me. One dress I especially remember was frilly pink with lots of material in the skirt. But the neatest thing was the pink satin sash that would cling to my waist like a belt. I twirled around in that dress thinking it was the most beautiful I had ever seen.

In our scripture today, God wants His people to cling to Him just like my pink sash did to my waist. He is our Heavenly Father and He likes us to stay close to Him.

1. What does it mean to cling to someone or something?

2. Do you have someone or something special you cling to?

3. Why would God want you and I to cling to Him?

It Was A Miracle

Luke 9:16a
"Then He (Jesus) took the five loaves and the two fish, and looking up to heaven He blessed and broke them..."

Seeing school buses always makes me think of the little school I attended. I especially remember lunchtime. I know you probably go to the cafeteria for lunch, but I had to take my lunch to school. I didn't have a fancy Barbie or Batman lunchbox. Mom wrapped my lunch in newspaper and tied it with a string.

I had never heard of pizza or chicken nuggets. I usually had a peanut butter or egg sandwich and some cookies. No milk. There was no way to keep the milk cold. All of us could get a drink of water outside after the lunch break was over. If we had chocolate covered grahams in our lunch the teacher allowed us to hold them over the furnace register and melt the chocolate. Mmmm, good. Of course, we had to go outside to the pump and wash our face and hands, but it was worth going out in the cold.

The Bible tells of a boy who had 5 barley loaves and 2 fish in his lunch and took it to a place where Jesus was teaching 5000 people. When lunchtime came his food was all they had for the people to eat. Jesus held the little boy's lunch up and thanked God for it. Through a great miracle, the lunch this little boy shared, was more than enough to feed all the people and have some left over.

1.   How do you think the boy felt at first when they took his lunch?

2.   He seemed willing to share. Do you share your things?

3.   Do you believe Jesus blesses us when we share what we have with others?

Going to the Store

Psalm 103:2

"Bless the Lord, O, my soul, and forget not all His benefits."

Dad was planning to go to John's Grocery in the little town of Terhune. He needed to go to the elevator. That meant we would be taking the tractor and wagon.

This was a real treat. Just riding in the wagon was oodles of fun. At the store, I remember walking on the squeaky, wooden floors. Mom liked to shop around when she came. We girls walked all the way to the back of the store where the meat counter was. Then we'd go to the glass cases full of candy. Choosing our favorite wasn't easy. So many decisions. There were candy coated raisins, cinnamon balls, tootsie rolls, candy corn, sugar coated orange slices, malted milk balls, and different kinds of hard candy. If Dad gave us a nickel, it was really hard to pick the candy we wanted.

Sometimes Dad had to look for a part to repair the tractor, or he'd need to go next door to the elevator to buy feed for the hogs. He sometimes gave us enough money for a cold pop and my sisters, and

I would sit on the porch and say "Hi" to everyone who came by. John's Grocery was a great place to visit. We were happy when Dad took us with him. He was a good dad.

God makes things like that happen for us. It's like a gift that encourages and makes us happy.

1. Why was this store such a fun place?

2. Is there a special fun place you go with your parents?

3. Do you know what it means to bless the Lord?

America's Birthday

John 8:36

"Therefore, if the Son makes you free, you shall be free indeed."

God Bless America! Land that we love. Every year, in July, we celebrate our country's birthday. It will take many, many candles for our country's birthday cake. Wow! Flags will be flying everywhere, and parades can be seen in the small towns and big cities. I'm proud to be an American, aren't you? People from all over the world want to come to America because they know it is a land of freedom.

We can be thankful, God allowed us to be born in a free country. Being free means we can run and play without being afraid. We can live in whatever town or city we choose. We can travel across many states and see all the beautiful sights. The mountains, the rivers, the oceans, the beautiful majestic buildings, the farmlands, and the big cities. There is much to see in our great land.

We can go to the church of our choice. We can pray and read our Bible. In some countries that is not allowed. Our country was founded by people who loved God and loved the freedom to worship. Let's pray that we will always have that freedom.

When you are older, you'll be free to vote for the country's leaders, like the President and the Governor. I hope you will remember all of these thoughts about freedom as you celebrate the Fourth of July. America truly is a beautiful land. Love it and learn all you can about your country. It is your home. Enjoy all the picnics and the fireworks as you celebrate.

1.   What does it mean to be free?

2.   What will you do to celebrate America's birthday?

3.   What makes our flag so special?

Time to do the Laundry

Proverbs 31: 13b,15b

"(She) willingly works with her hands and provides food for her household."

Monday morning was always a busy time because it was wash day. First, the water had to be carried in from the well outside and set on the stove to boil. (Washers and dryers had not been invented.) Our clothes were all gathered and sorted into piles. The nicer clothes went into the water first. Then sheets and towels followed by dark clothes and jeans. The water was kept so hot we had to use a stick to lift the clothes out and put them into the cold rinse water. it was a big job for Mom, and she was glad to have our help.

The rinse water was still clean. Mom used that water to mop the floor after we finished. Grabbing the bag of clothespins, we took the clothes out to the clothesline. Fastening them to the line they would dry in the summer breezes. If it was raining, Mom hung lines up in the long kitchen.

The smell of ham, beans, and cornbread cooking on the stove let us know we were going to have our favorite 'wash day' meal. Even with the washers and dryers today, doing laundry is still work. It will help your Mom if you keep your clean clothes picked up and your dirty laundry in the hamper. God always likes it when we do our part. We not only honor our parents, but we honor God as well.

1. How do you help Mom with the laundry?

2. The Bible says we are created to work. What if no one ever did any work?

3. Look around your house. Is there anything you can do to help?

What Do They Do with All That Milk?

1 Peter 2:2

"As newborn babes, desire the pure milk of the word, that you may grow..."

All cows have to be milked two times a day. I always wondered what happened to all that milk. Dad kept it in cold water in the milk house until the milk truck could pick it up. After taking the milk to the factory to be purified for drinking it ends up in the refrigerated cases at the grocery. People buy it by the gallons. Can you imagine not having milk?

It is so good for us. Babies, children, and grown-ups all drink milk. Children everywhere drink it for lunch at school. And just think of all the ways we use milk. We put it in cookies, cakes, pancakes, cornbread, muffins, and many other things we bake and cook. Milk is in yogurt and butter. It is also used to make cottage cheese as well as string cheese we like. Cows give us one of our most healthy foods.

God knew we would need milk when He created the cow. He compares His words in the Bible to milk because just as milk helps our bones grow strong, when we read the Bible it is like milk that helps us grow closer to Him.

1. Have you ever sat on a little stool and milked a cow?

2. Do you like white or chocolate milk best?

3. How is milk like God's word?

Music

Psalm 150: 3a,4b,5a

"Praise Him with the sound of the trumpet; Praise Him with stringed instruments; Praise Him with loud cymbals..."

The world is full of music. The birds sing, the wind whistles, the thunderclaps, and electrical wires hum. And people sing and play many different kinds of music on several different kinds of instruments.

Granny's first musical instrument was the piano. It was old but it sounded pretty when played. I had my very own book of songs to learn. I was so excited. But as the lessons went on, my songs were harder for me to play and I didn't like practicing as much. But my teacher and my mom were strict. They wouldn't let me give up. I am glad now they made me keep practicing.

Whether you are practicing piano, trumpet, violin, math facts, reading new words, hitting a baseball, kicking a ball, don't get discouraged and quit. The more you practice, the better you will become. I can promise you that.

The Bible tells us the angels sing praises to God. We, too, can praise God with our songs and instruments. All that we practice and do well, is a way for us to honor God.

1.   Do you have a special instrument you would like to learn to play?

2.   What do you do to make yourself keep practicing?

3.   Coyotes howling, cows mooing, chickens cheeping, horses whinnying; Do you think this is the animal's way of singing?

The Greatest Christmas Gift

Luke 2:7
"And she brought forth her first-born son, and wrapped Him in swaddling cloths, and laid Him in a manger..."

I know it is still November and we haven't had snow yet, but I'm getting excited about Christmas. How about you? It's only a few weeks away. Now is a good time to be thinking of the gifts we can make or buy for our family and friends. And we don't want to forget those who don't have much at Christmas.

Of course, once we get our gifts, we have to find just the right paper to wrap them. All those beautifully wrapped presents under the tree, always make us curious.

What kind of paper will you use to wrap your gifts? Will it be shiny red or gold color? Or will your paper have pictures of snowmen or Christmas bells, or maybe Santa riding in his sleigh?

On the very first Christmas, the greatest gift was not wrapped in pretty paper but wrapped in swaddling cloths and laying in a manger bed instead of under a tree. What was this great gift? The Baby Jesus! You might be wondering how Jesus is the greatest of all Christmas gifts. It is because our

Heavenly Father sent His only Son from heaven into our world to save us from sin, so that someday we could live forever with Him in heaven. Jesus is the One who makes Christmas so exciting. I hope it will be very exciting and happy for you this year.

1.   Why is Christmas so special to you?

2.   Is it possible to have Christmas without Jesus?

3.   Make a list of things you will do to help others during this Christmas season

My First Recital

Psalm 54:4
   "Behold, God is my helper."

It was the day of my first piano recital. I was nine years old. I would have to be on stage in front of many people and play the song I had been practicing for weeks. Even though I had the song memorized, I was really nervous. My stomach was turning flip flops.

I wore my new red skirt and sweater, with matching red socks. And Mom let me pick out my first pair of black patent leather shoes. I felt like a princess and twirled around trying to do a little tap dance.

Soon we were at the church and my teacher was introducing me and the song I was to play. Mom always helped me at home, but now I knew I was on my own. I also knew God would help me if I prayed. So, as I walked up on stage to the piano, I said a silent prayer that God would help me remember all the notes of my song. He did help me because I don't remember missing a note.

1.   Have you memorized a poem, your favorite scripture, or math facts?

2.   What do you think was Granny's favorite color?

3.   How does God help you when you have to do something special by yourself?

A Picnic in the Woods

Psalm 96:12b

"Then all the trees of the woods will rejoice before the Lord."

Don't you just love to go on a picnic? My friend Dottie lived just down the road. We could walk across the field to see each other. In the summer, we were always planning picnics in the woods.

We made sandwiches of bread and butter and sliced radishes. Sometimes it would be sliced dill pickles. We were happy when Mom made cookies for us. We had to walk a long lane to get to the woods. Once there, we headed straight for the creek and spread out a blanket on the grass. We laughed as we ran picking wildflowers to lay on the ground around our blanket.

Everyone called the creek, "Stink Creek" because the local milk factory washed the milk cans and let the water run into the creek. The hot sun would make the milk from the cans smell pretty bad. But we didn't let it bother us as we picnicked under the shade of the beautiful trees that God had made for us to enjoy. We always had a fun time.

1. Have you planned a picnic with your friend?

2. What will you fix to take on your picnic?

3. Where will you go for your picnic? (Make sure Mom or another adult will know where you are.)

Do Not Fear, Trust in God

Psalm 56:11

   "In God I have put my trust, I will not be afraid..."

Going out into the dark at night was so scary for Granny. My knees would shake, and my heart would beat so fast. I ran to do what I had to do and then ran back to the house as fast as I could go. If I heard an owl hooting, I would run even faster.

It was a great day when Dad decided to put a pole light in the lot between the house and the barn. The light was so bright it lit up part of the orchard. Now we could go out of doors on warm summer evenings, after dark, and not be afraid.

God tells us many times in the Bible to not be afraid. We really do have to put our trust in Him. He will always take care of us.

1.   Have you ever had to run fast because you were afraid of something?

2.   What is there about the dark that makes us afraid?

3.   Looking back at the story, what does God tell us to do?

Cleaning My Toenails

Ephesians 6:2-3
"Honor your father and mother, which is the first commandment with promise, that it may be well with you and you may live long on the earth."

Remember, kids sometimes do crazy things. We don't always stop and think. That's why God gives us Moms and Dads to help us. It was time to think about supper. Mom brought a big bowl of potatoes out to the back porch. Our big family loved fried potatoes. I began peeling and peeling. After a few minutes, I got bored and began looking around and stopped peeling. It was a warm, summer day and I was barefoot. My toenails were awfully dirty. So, I put my foot up on the step and began cleaning my toenails. That wasn't a bad thing to do, but I was using the same knife peeling the potatoes.

I heard the back door open and Mom said very crossly, "You can't use that knife to clean your toenails. Get a clean knife and get those potatoes peeled. It's getting late!" I didn't understand what all the fuss was about, but I did as I was told and finally got that bowl of potatoes peeled. The grownups laughed about what I had done for a long time.

When Mom and Dad have to scold for something you did, just listen and learn from it. God knew, as children, we would need a little guidance now and then. I thank God that he gave me good parents that helped me to grow into a kind, caring person. He will help you too, if you will remember our verse of scripture for today.

1. Do you have a story about something you did that was funny?

2. Why was it so wrong for Granny to clean her toenails with the same knife?

3. What do you do when you get bored at a job you have to do?

Pigs and the Son
Who Was Sorry?

Luke 15:13

"...the younger son... journeyed to a far country, and there wasted his possessions on prodigal (wrong) living."

The barn on our farm was a great shelter for the animals. It was shady and cool in the summer and nice and warm in the winter. The pigs had their place in the back of the barn. They loved the corn we threw into their pen each evening. But my, they were messy and smelly. Whew! Rude and noisy too. They would oink, oink so much, we could hardly hear. They thought nothing of wallowing in the mud and then coming in the barn to eat. I didn't like being around the pigs or having to clean their pen. Yuck!

In the Bible, Jesus tells of the Prodigal Son who didn't like pigs either. He had left his home and wasted all the money his father had given him. He found a job feeding a farmer's pigs. He had gone days without eating. He thought the pig's food looked good enough to eat. That's when he began to realize he had not been nice to his father. He decided to go home and tell him he was sorry for what he had done.

Because his father loved his son so much, he forgave him and even had a party for him. He was glad his son had come home.

Our Father, God, is like that. We sometimes do things that we know we shouldn't. We have to ask Him to forgive us for being selfish and disrespectful. God loves us and will help us do what is right if we pray and ask Him.

1. What else might you find in a big barn?

2. Why did the Prodigal Son decide to go back home?

3. Have you ever had to say you were sorry for something you had done?

Riding Our Bike

Acts 10:38

"(*Jesus*)... *went about doing good...for God was with Him.*"

School was out for the day. I couldn't wait to get home and ride the bike. It was an old bike with more than a few rust spots and none of the fancy gears that bikes have today. I had to share rides with my two sisters, but I knew we would have fun.

We ran to the house, all out of breath, excited to be home. As soon as we walked in the back door, we knew Mom had a totally different plan for us. Bummers! She had been canning tomato juice all day. She was tired and grumpy. She needed help cleaning up. We wanted to fuss but knew if we talked back, we would get a spanking. Talking back to our parents was not allowed. So, we did what Mom asked.

We didn't get to ride our bikes that evening. But there were many other evenings when we did ride. We would take off from the barn, build up speed, and coast down the big hill. Feeling the air blowing our hair and cooling our faces was the best fun a kid could have on a warm September evening.

Jesus didn't have a bike to ride. He had to walk everywhere. Sometimes He got in a boat. The Bible says He went about doing good. I know He, too, must have enjoyed the cool breezes blowing off the Sea of Galilee as He walked and prayed for the people. When you help your Mom or Dad you are doing something good, just like Jesus.

1. What is most fun for you after being at school all day?

2. Why is it not good to "talk back" to our parents or our teachers?

3. Think of 3 things you have done this week that was doing good.

Sing A New Song

Psalm 40:3

"He has put a new song in my mouth-Praise to our God;"

I love to sing, do you? When I was young like you, I would sit on a stump in the front yard and sing to the birds, the dog, the cat, anyone who was out of doors to listen. When my brother and I drove the cows up from the pasture to the barn, I would sing to them. I sang as I fed the baby chicks. They would cheep-cheep and sing right along with me.

Singing makes me happy. It chases away my fears. It helps me when I'm not feeling the best. Even my sad thoughts are carried far away when I sing. The Bible says God has put a new song in our mouth. He does that so we can praise Him. In Psalm 96:1, He tells us to sing a new song to the Lord, sing it everywhere…sing out His praises. He wants us to sing with joy every day, even when we don't feel like it. Sing to the Lord because He has blessed you so much. (Psalm 13:6)

So, when you are in church, in Kid's Klub, or Awana, and it's time for music, that's your special moment to praise God for all that He has done for you. Sing out, don't be shy. If you think your voice sounds funny, don't worry. God loves to hear you singing when you are praising Him.

1. What kind of music do you like best?

2. Do you like to have someone sing to you at bedtime?

3. Try making up your own songs to sing to God and thank Him for His many blessings.

Honoring Our Parents

Ephesians 6:2-3

"Honor your father and mother, which is the first commandment with promise; that it may be well with you and you may live long on the earth."

My sisters and I shivered as we climbed out of bed. The cold floor woke up our toes as we quickly headed for the stairs. Sleeping in the upstairs of our three-story brick farmhouse was great in the summertime. The cool breezes blew in the windows and we could hear crickets chirping to one another. But during the month of February it was much different. The cold winds of winter found every little crack and crevice to blow through and make us shiver and shake until we got under the covers. When it was really snowing hard, we would wake up to find a dusting of snow on our blankets. Brrrr! That was cold!

We hurried down the stairs in our flannel pajamas to warm ourselves beside the pot-bellied stove in the kitchen. Dad always built a warm fire before he went to the barn to milk the cows. I'm glad we helped him by bringing up the coal from the basement.

The Bible tells us to honor our parents for all the things they do for us. He has a special promise for us if we do.

1. Since it is cold in winter, do you find fun things to do inside? Name some.

2. Can you think of a time when you shivered and shook from the cold?

3. Did you find the promise God gives in this verse?

Sledding in the Snow

Job 37:6
"For He (God) says to the snow, fall on earth;"

Snowy January days always take me back to another time. I hear the putt-putt-putt of the tractor. Yay! Dad had the sled hooked to the tractor and ready to go. He yelled to us, "Anybody want to go for a ride?" We were excited. Putting on warm coats, hats, mittens, and boots, we'd jump on the sled and away we would go.

I can still hear the sound of the crunching snow and feel the sting of the flakes as they hit my nose and rested on my eyelashes. We'd stop at the neighbors and pick up our friends. Sledding along the road, the snow blowing into our faces made us laugh. If we fell off the sled, no worry. There was usually enough snow on the road we didn't get hurt. We were having so much fun, we hoped it would last forever. But it wasn't long before we began to feel the cold creeping into our warm gloves and mittens and biting our fingers and toes. Dad turned the tractor and sled around and headed home. Back at the house, we warmed up around the wood stove, drinking some of Mom's hot cocoa. It had sure been a fun day.

I wonder how much snow God will give us this winter. Hmm! I hope it is enough that we can go sledding, don't you? The Bible tells us God has a treasury of snow. Ask someone to help you find the scripture about that. That sounds like a lot of snow.

1. What do you do on snowy days?

2. Is snow good for other things besides sledding?

3. Name 5 things you can do with snow.

Snowballs

Proverbs 23:12

"Apply your heart to instruction and your ears to words of knowledge."

Is it really time for school to be starting? Is summer over so soon? That's probably what you are thinking too. On the first day of school, there are always so many rules to be learned. We have to really make our ears listen. When I was in first grade, there was a time I didn't listen. I wanted to do my own thing.

It was the first big snow and the teacher told us not to go to the far end of the playground, because the boys would be building forts and throwing snowballs. (Throwing snowballs is not allowed at school today.) My problem was; the big slide I loved to play on, was at the far end of the playground. I really wanted to slide so I went all by myself. I climbed the ladder looking forward to the slide down. Just as I got to the top, WHAM! right on my head. I backed down, crying all the way back to the school building. The teacher came running. "What happened?" she asked.

"I got hit with a snowball," I cried, pointing to my head.

"Did you listen when I told you not to go where the boys were playing in their forts?" she scolded.

My teacher was very nice, but she didn't have much sympathy for me because I didn't listen to her instructions, the scripture verse today tells us to listen and obey. I learned the hard way, a very important lesson that day.

1.   I loved to slide, but what should I have done?

2.   Was the teacher mad at me or disappointed that I hadn't listened?

3.   Can you think of a time when you didn't listen? Did you get in trouble?

Wet Mittens

Deuteronomy 28:6
"Blessed shall you be when you come in and blessed shall you be when you go out."

Snowy days always remind me of wet mittens. I recall the radiators that stood along the wall of my classroom at our three-room school. The radiators were the heaters that kept our school warm. You are wondering what that has to do with wet mittens.

During recess, the girls rolled big snowballs to see who could build the biggest snowman. The boys were always busy building a snow fort. By the time recess was over, our mittens were soaked, and our hands were freezing. When the bell rang, we walked into the room and went straight to the radiators and put our wet mittens on top so they could dry before next recess.

It was such a simple thing. The heat from the radiators dried our mittens and warmed our cold fingers and toes. God made sure there were people who brought the coal and kept the radiators heating and warming our school on those cold snowy days. That was truly a special blessing for us.

1. What do snowy days remind you of?

2. Do you have a favorite "snowy day" game you play at recess?

3. How has God blessed you?

Baby Chick

Psalm 17:8
"Keep me as the apple of Your eye; Hide me under the shadow of Your wings."

Springtime always reminds me of baby chicks. They are so cute, soft, and cuddly. Mom and Dad always bought the chicks at the Hatchery in town. They came in boxes with little holes in the side of the box so the chicks could get air to breathe.

There was always much to be done before they arrived. First, we had to get the 'brooder house' ready for 200 of those little cheepers. Like all babies it was important for them to have a clean, warm place. To keep them warm, a big metal lamp hung from the ceiling about 10 inches from the floor. The light of the lamp gave enough heat to keep the babies toasty warm. Just as though they were under the wings of the mother hen. Sometimes the baby chicks would peck each other instead of their food. Mom would have to put medicine on their sore places. The medicine didn't taste good. That made them quit pecking each other.

When we put out food and water for them, they would be so happy, they would all start running around cheeping. It was so much fun to watch them hurry and scurry about. But like you, they didn't stay babies very long.

God tells us in the Bible, we can hide under the shadow of His wings. And just like the mother hen protects her little ones, God will protect us. I like that idea, don't you?

1. What do you think it means to "hide under the shadow of God's wings?"

2. Have you ever held a baby chick? How did they feel?

3. Why is it so important to be gentle and loving with all babies?

Pleasing God in Our Work

Psalm 126:2

"Then our mouth was filled with laughter, and our tongue with singing."

March and April bring happy thoughts of spring. It was going to be great not to have to put on heavy coats and boots every day. We couldn't wait. But before my sisters and I could get too excited about being out in the sunshine and spending our days swinging and riding our bike, we had to help with the spring cleaning.

Burning wood and coal, during the cold winter, made a lot of dust and dirt in the house. The carpets needed a good sweeping. The wallpaper had to be wiped down with something that looked like play-dough. The curtains had to be washed and dried. And the baseboard needed a good scrubbing. The windows had to be cleaned. That was a big job because there were a lot of windows in the big brick house where Granny grew up.

Doing all that work wasn't much fun but Mom always encouraged us to laugh and sing as we worked, and our work would go much faster. And it did. Our

Mom was very wise. She knew that doing our work without grumbling would please God.

1. When you help Mom with the work, do you think God likes that?

2. What do you do to help Mom with cleaning?

3. How does laughing and singing help to get our work done?

Spring Storms

Mark 4:37-38a

"And a great windstorm arose, and the waves beat into the boat, so that it was already filling, But He (Jesus) was in the stern, asleep on a pillow..."

Spring will soon be here and along with it, warm and rainy days. I'm as anxious as you are for those warm days, but spring can also bring storms. That means high winds, beating rain, hail, thunder, and lightning. Storms can be very scary.

The disciples were in a boat with Jesus. They were on the Sea of Galilee, when a terrible storm came up. The waves got bigger and bigger and water started washing over the sides of the boat. The disciples were frightened. What if the water washed them overboard? What if their boat sank? Where was Jesus?

He was, of all things, sound asleep! They shook Him awake, shouting, "DON'T YOU CARE THAT WE MIGHT DROWN?" They were very afraid. Jesus got up and spoke. He told the wind and the waves to be still and for the sea to be calm and peaceful. He told His disciples not to be afraid but to have faith. He would take care of them.

When we hear the weatherman tell us that a bad storm is coming, we should go to safe places, but we should also pray and believe that God will watch over us until all is calm and the sun is shining again.

1. Do you know where the safe places are in your home?

2. What do you do to help yourself when frightened?

3. Draw a picture of your house and all the safe places.

The State Fair

Romans 15:13

"...*may the God of hope fill you with all joy...*"

Going to the State Fair was one of the best times of my growing up years. I know it was a lot of work for Mom and Dad, but they did their best to make it a fun day for the whole family. We took blankets for a picnic. And water and lots of good food: fried chicken, potato salad, bread and butter sandwiches, and usually chocolate cake. Yum! There were six of us, so it took a lot of food.

We woke up early and were usually there by 9 o'clock. Dad still had to park the car a long way from where we actually went in. We passed the Midway with all the colorful lights and rides. We'd come back later for a few rides. But now we were going to see the cows, sheep, horses, pigs, and, of course, Mom wanted to see the quilts and all the other things that grown-ups like to see.

It was a long day because we usually stayed till Dad had to be home to milk the cows. I know we were pretty tired and probably went to sleep on the way home. Going to the State Fair was an exciting time.

157

God likes for us to have fun. We are His children and He enjoys seeing us be joyful and happy.

1. Do you have a special family activity?

2. What do you like to do that makes you the happiest?

3. 3.What can you do this day that will make someone else happy?

The Great Taffy Pull

Ecclesiastes 3:11

"He (God) has made everything beautiful in its time."

Mary was one of my friends in second grade. She lived in a little town not too far from the farm where I lived. I loved going to her house and spending the night. There were so many fun things to do.

Mary had a paper route. When I was there, I would go with her to deliver the papers and sometimes the people would give us a couple pennies to put in our pocket. We could buy lots of different kinds of candy for a penny in those days.

Mary's mom would have taffy made when we got back to the house. We buttered our hands and pulled the taffy till it was just right to eat. Of course, we giggled a lot and smacked our sticky hands together. It was messy, but lots of fun.

This summer pray that God will show you creative ways to have fun. Turn off the TV and the video games and let your imagination stir up some fun activities to do. God has made the out of doors so beautiful for us. We need to enjoy every day of summer.

1. What are some fun things you can do with friends? Family?

2. Jesus didn't have TV or even a radio. What do you think He did for fun?

3. Put on a play, write a poem or song, ride your bike, look for pretty rocks, look at the clouds, play with your pets. Run! Walk! Jump! Have fun!

People and Animals Share the Earth

Genesis 1:21-26
  "So, God created... every living thing that moves...And
God saw that it was good."

Is this going to be a good summer? Will you be riding your bike, going swimming, reading a good book, or maybe going camping with your family? I liked swinging high in the treetops, riding in the cart with Billy Goat pulling us down the lane, picnicking at the park, and playing kickball with the neighbors. I always liked summer.

Summer was also great for exploring on the farm where I lived. I once found a corner in our orchard where there were bushes and trees all around. I noticed the tall grass was all mashed down. Dad said a deer family had been there through the winter, maybe even had their babies there in the spring.

Wow! I kept watching every day to see if they would come back. But I never saw them that summer. They must have found safe woods to live in. A place where people wouldn't find them.

God created many different kinds of animals to live on the earth with us. And they each have a purpose just like you and me.

1. How many different kinds of animals can you name?

2. Is summer your favorite of the four seasons?

3. Can you find in the first chapter of the Bible the person who named all the animals?

Thanksgiving

Psalm 100:4

"Enter into His gates with thanksgiving...Be thankful to Him and bless His name."

'Over the river and through the woods to Grandmother's house we go.'

And oh, the fun we would have. All the cousins, too many to count, would be there. We could hardly wait for this day to arrive.

Granny lived in a big, big, house that had a big, big room upstairs. Since it was usually too cold on Thanksgiving to play out of doors, the grown-ups sent us upstairs to play. We didn't have a lot of toys, so we all came up with ideas. Sometimes, there were arguments over whose idea was best.

Usually, the girls played house with their dolls and the boys played like they were cowboys. They were always sneaking into our corner scaring us. Of course, we all screamed so loud that it brought the adults running to see what had happened.

We never ran out of things to do. We built tents, played board games, jumped on the bed, (Shhh! Don't tell.) and made up our own little plays. Soon it was time for turkey and noodles and mashed potatoes. Yum! Yum!

This Thanksgiving, we can all be thankful for family and the good times we have together. And don't forget to pray and thank God for His many blessings.

1. What do you do on Thanksgiving?

2. Why do we celebrate this special day?

3. Name six things you are thankful for.

Towser

1 Timothy 4:4a
    "For every creature of God is good..."

He was such a beautiful puppy. He had long, brownish golden hair that glistened when he was in the sun. Dad had found him along the side of the road and brought him home. We kids were jumping with excitement, talking at the same time about what we would name our new pet. We finally chose the name, 'Towser.'

Towser would be a farm dog so he wasn't allowed in the house. We fixed him a special place under the porch out of bad weather. Towser went everywhere with us. When we took a blanket out under the trees and sat down with our toys to play, he would grab our toys and take off with them. He wanted us to chase him. When we rode our bikes down the lane to get the mail, he followed along. If we went inside, he would stand at the door and wait for us. We loved Towser and he loved us.

When Towser grew up, he had to help herd the cows and get the unruly hogs into the truck for market. He couldn't understand why chasing after the chickens wasn't part of his job too. He loved to see them running and squawking. Towser was a loving dog and very smart. We took turns giving him food and water every day. I hope you do the same for your pets. God created all of our pets and He wants us to take good care of them.

1. Do you have a favorite pet?

2. What kind of pet would be easier for you to care for: a cat, a dog, a camel?

3. Animals have feelings like people. They get afraid. They get their feelings hurt. They need love. What else do you know about animals?

Visiting My Cousins

Romans 15:13
"Now may the God of hope fill you with all joy..."

It was time for me to spend a week with my cousins. I was so excited. They planned wonderful fun things to do. It was in the summer and usually hot. One of the first things we did was go to the garden and cut rhubarb and eat it sprinkled with salt. Rhubarb is like eating really sour candy. We thought it was a lip-smacking treat. We sat in the porch swing and talked about school and fun things while we ate. Sometimes we would eat ice cubes or green apples with salt. And then, there were mulberries to pick and eat. We could always find a snack.

Some days we walked down to the bridge and watched the fish swimming around. It was our job every day to walk down the road to get the mail. That gave us a lot of time to talk and share stories. Of course, we played house with our dolls.

Their dog, Tippy, followed us everywhere we went. Their yard had two trees that were just perfect for climbing because they weren't very tall. We never fell once. The week ended much too soon. I had to go home. It was sad to leave my cousins and all the fun we had, but Mom told me to be thankful for the time we had to play and be together. She was right. We should always be thankful for the good things God gives us.

1. Do you have cousins that live far away?

2. Have you stayed overnight or longer with them?

3. Did you get homesick?

Haymaking Days

Matthew 14:19b

"And He took the five loaves and the two fish, and looking up to heaven, He blessed and broke and gave the loaves to the disciples..."

June was a busy month on the farm. All the grownups were up early.

The neighbors who helped each other would gather at one farm and prepare to cut the hay and get it lifted up into the big room above the barn. That room was called the haymow or hayloft.

The moms all gathered in the kitchen to cook the noon meal. The kitchen would be steaming hot. There was no air conditioning. But our moms didn't let the heat stop them. They knew the men would be hungry. Ham, fried chicken, bowls of potatoes, gravy, green beans, slaw, and delicious rolls would be ready. Pie was always a favorite dessert.

We kids had lots of time to play but we also had to do our part. We learned to set the table the right way. We pumped water in buckets for the men to wash off the dust from the hay. And while the men were eating, we made sure they had plenty of water to drink. We were hungry and the food smelled so good, but we knew we had to wait and eat with our moms after the men finished their meal. We were afraid there would not be enough food left over but there was always plenty.

1. Does this story make you think of Jesus feeding the five thousand? In what way?

2. Do you think those people thought the food would all be gone?

3. How many baskets of leftovers did they have? Isn't God good?

King and Queenie

Jeremiah 4:13b
    "His horses are swifter that eagles."

Are you ready for spring? The animals are dancing and frolicking in the fields. They are happy about spring, just like us. I like to watch the horses and the baby colts. They are God's beautiful creations.

When I was five-year-old, we had two farm horses named King and Queenie. They helped Dad with the field work and other chores. Queenie was the most gentle. My sisters and I were always begging to ride Queenie.

One warm April day, Dad decided, we could ride. He put all three of us on Queenie and led us back to the pasture where he had to repair a broken gate. We sat on Queenie and waited. Queenie must have had a fly bite her leg because she stomped her foot. We thought she was taking off. We began yelling," Whoa!" That scared Queenie and she started moving. All three of us fell "plop' to the ground. When we fell, Queenie stopped still. She seemed to know not to step on us. We weren't hurt, just a little frightened. I can't remember riding a horse again until I was much older, but I still remember that ride when we all fell off.

The Bible has a lot to say about horses. King David's son, Solomon, had many horses that pulled chariots and were swifter than eagles. I'm glad Queenie wasn't that fast.

1. Have you ever ridden on a horse?

2. What is your favorite animal?

3. Write 5 ways that horses help people.

Author Lora Goff was born in a small farming community near Lebanon, Indiana. At two years of age her mother passed away and her life changed dramatically. She moved in with her oldest sister and family. Her love for God at an early age, along with the values she was taught, has influenced her writing.

Lora is a graduate of Indiana University with a Masters in Elementary Education. She retired after teaching for thirty-three years in the public schools. She has taught classes on How to Write Your Life Story/Memoir Writing. She now spends time writing, visiting with those who are homebound and/or in nursing home facilities. She also volunteers at a local hospital and teaches a weekly in-depth Bible Study at her church.

Lora's writings have been published in "Light from the Word", a daily devotional of the Wesleyan Publishing House, the "Good Old Days" magazine, as well as articles in the county newspaper. She also writes a daily blog; 'Hope in God Devotionals".

Lora is a member of the Noblesville, Indiana Writer's Group and the Westfield, Indiana Writer's Group.

Lora and her late husband, Rollie, have four grown children, six grandchildren, and two great-grandchildren. She loves writing, music, watching football, walking, and being with family. She resides near Westfield, Indiana.